Experience of Life

Vs.

Expert Advice

Nataisha T. Hill

Published by TaiLorMade Books

Dedication

This book is dedicated to ones whom I love best. I am forever devoted to my loving mom, family, and true friends who have stuck beside me through all trials and tribulations. Last, but definitely not least, my Loving God, who gives me strength, wisdom, intelligence, patience, meekness, kindness, temperance, loyalty, and everything that makes me who I am.

Chapter 1
The Introduction

Nowadays it seems as if more and more people are seeking "expert" relationship advice when it comes to their relationship. Normally, expert advice consists of professionals who perhaps studied at accredited colleges or universities for several years on particular psychological and behavioral interactions in relationships. Credit is given where credit is due. I too, studied sociology and psychology at a community college as well as Middle Tennessee State University, but to be honest, my thoughts, opinions, and conclusions regarding relationships mainly came from one source, life itself. Everyone wants to be the expert when it comes to relationships. We all have theories on what should or should not exist when two people decide to be in a committed union. Some experts say that the relationship your parents have when you are a child directly affects the relationship you have with someone as an adult. While this may be true in a sense, I think it is what it is-just an expert opinion.

In actuality, isn't all relationship advice an opinion? Isn't there always going to be a situation that totally defies what an expert may say? I wrote this book to give people different perspectives on relationships, not to necessarily imply that situations in this book apply to them. Some of them don't even apply to me. Overall, I hope readers gain insight and perhaps can relate or find ways to improve their overall happiness.

A short introduction of myself, I am a thirty-two year old married woman with a four-year college degree and two adorable daughters. My days consist of bottles, diapers, and nap time for my infant and homework, dolls, and playtime for my six-year old. I've known my husband for over twenty years since we met in middle school. For the most part, I can definitely say we compliment each other. We share the same ideas, concepts, and values regarding life.

We love, care, and respect one another, which is vital in the growth of a marriage. Nevertheless, as with any relationship, we have our share of disagreements and we are constantly learning ways to overcome negative circumstances. Fights and disagreements in a relationship are inevitable. Arguments can be as small as who does the dishes tonight or what detergent do we use for washing the clothes. The only way to prevent an altercation is not have an opinion or ignore the traditions and values that your parents or guardians taught you. At some point an argument will ensue, which is why it's important to get to know your mate before jumping into something serious.

Before one reaches marriage, as with most cultures, dating must occur. Dating is the process where you get to know someone on a personal level. It's the stage where you are suppose to learn likes and dislikes, what turns your partner on and off, what makes them happy, sad, mad, or indifferent. It's the stage where you indulge in the essence of your partner. You may ask yourself, what if I don't want to know anything about this person? What if I just want to use the person I'm with for sex, money, or any other selfish indulgence? Then clearly, reading about dating and marriage may not interest you. However, before you put this book down you may want to ask yourself if you are actually the one being used while assuming you are the user. Yes, people, this does happen.

I had a friend back in college who messed around with this guy, who we will call Joe, only to make her ex-boyfriend jealous. She had no true intentions of seriously dating Joe; she just wanted to be seen with him by her ex lover. They had a few short phone conversations, back and forth texts, and at home movie nights.

After sleeping with him a few times, she took pictures of them and "accidently" sent them to her ex lover. Meanwhile, Joe thought he had the upper hand because he only called her at night when he intended to have sex with her. He never asked her on a real date, took her around his friends, or tried to get to know personal things about her. My friend didn't care because she really only wanted her ex back. Long story short, my friend did end up back with her ex and Joe, the late night creeper, was instantly cut off. Ironically, Joe had gotten comfortable with his arrangement and wasn't ready to let her go. It's probably fair to say that sex made Joe develop unintentional intimate feelings, but the moral of the story is, "you" may be the one getting the short end of the stick while assuming you have it made.

For those who are interested in having a real relationship stimulated by a deep connection, how do you know if the one you're with is on the same page? Unfortunately, sometimes you can't tell because people can be very deceitful. However, all things are revealed with time and there are always signs to help determine a person's sincerity.

Chapter 2

How do you know if your mate is interested?

How do you know when your partner is interested in you, but not too interested? Well, this can be tricky since everyone is usually on his or her best behavior in the beginning. One thing I've noticed about a guy who's interested in me is that even after a couple of months dating, he'll still make plans for us to do things together. He'll know when and what time the new movie I wanted to see starts and what is going on downtown afterwards. Rather going to a barbeque at his friend's house, going out to dinner, or a walk in the park, he'll make plans to be with you even when he's already with you. Makes sense? Another thing I've noticed about a guy who's interested is that he really pays attention to the small things such as what colors you wear, things you like to eat, your favorite songs and television shows.

True story: I talked to a guy back in college and we had an early morning class together.

We were listening to one of our usual early morning lectures when my stomach began to growl. He looked at me and jokingly said, "You're not hungry are you?" I laughed and said, "I never get a chance to fix myself breakfast because I'm always running late." We talked on the phone that same night and there was no mention of me being hungry in class that morning. At the beginning of our next class session, he handed me a breakfast bar and told me he brought it because he knew I probably didn't have time to fix breakfast.

This is obviously a small ordeal, but it's considerate things like this that matter. There will be other signs that he's interested too, such as he may leave sweet little messages or thoughtful gifts. A big sign would be him wanting you to hang out with his family. Men who are interested are normally consistent with calling, even if it's just to make sure you made it safely to a destination after a long drive, or after hanging out with your girlfriends. He'll want to know that you are okay in hopes of seeing you later on that night, the next day, or whenever he can.

Last but not least, pay attention to how he talks to you and that'll tell you everything. Does he tell you you're beautiful or constantly talk about how pretty that video model is opposed to you? Does he thank you for the things you do for him or does he complain about what you don't do? Does he tell you to keep your head up when you're having a bad day at work or does he even ask about your day at all? Don't forget, avoiding the small details may affect how you handle ending the courtship. It's much easier to leave a person when you know they aren't very interested in the first place. However, and I'm speaking only to the ladies, if you have a good man then you should also show and tell him how much you appreciate him, because, I promise, "Jane" will be right around the corner, whispering in his ear.

If men are reading this book, which I hope they are, how do you tell if a woman is interested? To be honest guys, in the beginning, women can be interested or pretend to be interested in you for multiple reasons. She could have heard that you have a nice "package" downstairs or she knows (or thinks) you have money, and as I mentioned earlier, women may pretend to be interested just to spite an ex-lover or even another female. While there are genuine woman out here, in my personal opinion, it's harder to tell a woman's true interest because, truth be told, a woman will stick with a man just because it's convenient for her lifestyle. For example, a woman may not be pleased with her man's lovemaking, but she will stick with him because he is good with her kids or she doesn't have to work. Perhaps its vice-versa, maybe he is good in bed, but has no work ethic whatsoever.

Honestly, men, it's hard to tell, but I can say this about some of the women I personally know. The women I know who love their men take time to talk about things their men are interested in. They keep themselves looking and smelling good for their men. They cook, clean, wash clothes, and whatever else is needed around the home. They buy their men nice gifts, they treat their men with respect and loyalty, and finally, yet importantly, they make love to their men, even if they are pissed off at them. Now that's real.

Chapter 3
Courting

It has been two weeks since you and that special someone went out on your first date. Things seemed as if they went great, but you haven't heard from them. Is this you? Have you ever wondered why that certain guy or girl didn't call you back after the date, if the physical attraction was mutual and it wasn't a blind date? What could have possibly gone wrong? Here are a few possible reasons why you didn't receive that call.

All About You…Have you ever gone on a first date with someone that was more interested in his or herself than you were? I know I have, and if you haven't, you may be the person described in this example. One of the biggest mistakes made on a first date is to engage in too much self-talk. This could extend from talking too much about your likes and dislikes to bragging about your accomplishments.

I went out with a guy who talked for forty-five minutes about his fraternity and how wild their parties were. It wasn't that the stories were boring, or bad, but that's all I learned about him. I couldn't really remember the other five or ten minutes of other interests and aversions. There has to be some type of equilibrium. Once your date asks you a question, answer that specific question and not five extras that were irrelevant to the subject at hand. Then, it would be a good idea to ask them something similar in order to shift the attention to them. Kind of like a game of verbal volleyball. In addition to this, no one wants to hear about all the extreme **relationships** with your ex-lovers. Leave your dramatic experiences at the precinct where they belong.

Forwardness…Being forward on date simply means pushing a circumstance beyond its normal boundaries or jumping too far ahead of what constitutes typical first-date standards. This could be trying to force a kiss on your date, insisting that your date goes home with you, or making plans for your date to meet your parents the same night.

Men and women both can be forward on a first date. For instance, when a man is forward in regards to sex, he comes off as being too aggressive, so typically a woman assumes that sex is all he is after. Likewise, if a woman is too forward, again in regards to sex, she may be perceived as being too promiscuous and could come off as a cheap thrill to a man. If you are interested in your date, you should take it slow. Discover what is appealing to that person and the things that person detests. All the things will align naturally if the vibe is good between you two.

Distractions…There is nothing more important on a first date than giving your date your undivided attention. This means turning your phone on vibrate and taking care of business calls before the date. If, for some reason, you feel you must accept a call, make it brief. I would also recommend that you don't walk away from your date to answer. Why? Well, who wants to seem as if they have something to hide? In addition to cell phone distractions, don't get caught checking out the hot waitress or handsome waiter across the room.

Even though your date may not mention that they saw you checking that person out, they were probably paying more attention than you realize. This is especially true with women because we notice almost every woman in our area who is attractive way before our date does. Therefore, keep in mind not to utilize the wondering eyes. I hope that your date has dressed appealing enough to keep your attention.

Types of relationships

There are so many ways to define a relationship. You have open relationships, serious relationships, and non-existent **relationships**. A non-existent-relationship is when one partner assumes he or she is with the other person after a few phone conversations, dates, and/or sex. This is one reason why it is important for you to know what you are trying to have or build with a person at the beginning of a courtship. Although not everyone you meet may be honest when you first start courting him or her, always ask regardless.

Personally, I wouldn't start a first date conversation with, "Are you eventually trying to marry me or not?" However, I would ask that person where they are relationship wise in their life. You may also want to ask them where they are in life in general because if they are still in the stage of trying to figure out who they are and what they want, then fifty percent of the focus that should be building the relationship is going right back to them. Trust me, you'll spend more time playing "super hero" than you will mutually getting to know one another, but that's a different discussion.

Getting back to the subject at hand, you can ask if they are just mingling, trying to settle down, or just trying to have sex. Omit the last one unless you are just that bold. A common response that many men give is, "Well, I'm just chilling and hanging out, but when the right woman comes along then I may settle down." Women, do not make the common mistake of automatically assuming you are that "right woman" no matter how pretty or thoughtful you think you are.

Although there is a possibility you could be the right one, judging from his statement, you are just an option at that time with the possibility of being upgradeable.

Not surprisingly, but not too many men ask women this question because most men know the traditional woman is looking for commitment or marriage in the long run. Notice I did use the term "traditional" woman.

Chapter 4&5
The Relationship

From time to time, I hear men and women say that a relationship is always better in the beginning. I hear women say that their men were more aware of them physically and emotionally when first dating, while some men say that their women were more aware of themselves physically and emotionally. This can be contributed to the fact that some people, both male and female, put on their best behavior in order to impress their newly found companion.

This is done to reach whatever intentions each individual has in regards to the relationship, such as love, finances, sex, or any other possibilities that one may acquire from a relationship. It's a natural thing. The question is what do you do when the two of you mutually have true love as your intentions, but the relationship gets dull or not as exciting as it once was in the beginning? Here are a few pointers that might ignite that old spark.

Getting the spark back…One simple answer is to never stop treating that person as you did in the beginning. The key to this simple step is to have continuous flirtation throughout the day. Do you remember that cute "I miss you" text that you once sent in the beginning, well don't just remember it, keep sending it. Shower your mate with an upgrade to the compliments that you gave in the beginning. Spend time role-playing as if you never met and you're dating for the first time. It may sound silly, but you'll be surprised by the results it will bring.

Do something unusual…This could be something that you've never done before. If you truly enjoy the person you're with, step outside the box and discover a boundary never crossed before. For instance, if you are a guy, but not the type of guy to send flowers to your woman's job, go even above and beyond and send a private gift basket to her job filled with things that she enjoys. If you are a woman, but not the type of woman that wears make-up, surprise your man with a full makeover including attire that he has never or rarely sees you in regularly.

Travel together…This could extend from a day or two or a few days. Go someplace where you two can have private conversations not involving work or other stresses of life. Enjoy one another on a mental, spiritual, physical, and emotional level. In addition to this, play card or **board games** throughout the week as well as participate in outside activities. It's enough that most of us have to stay on an unchanging nine to five work schedule, so it is important not to put your relationship on a schedule as well. There has to be spontaneity in order to keep it exciting.

True love…Let's discuss the subject of true love. How do you know when it is true love between you and your partner? Well, honestly this is a subject with constant variables and can be extremely circumstantial; however, the first obvious answer is that the two of you are exclusive, meaning that no one is dating anyone else outside of the relationship. With me, personally, it always was a hit and miss. Either I was in love with him, but he wasn't in love with me or vice-versa. However, I can tell you what constitutes true love and its qualifications.

The first qualification would be that both people would mutually wake up thinking about one another. They would enjoy being with one another on a regular basis while respecting each other's space. In addition to this, they would praise and celebrate one another's accomplishments, and be there to comfort one another when disappointments occur. If there is a misunderstanding or argument, and there will be one at some point in the relationship, both parties will hear each other complaints instead of talking over the other or trying to manipulate the opposing partner's point of view in order to get them to comply with what they are saying.

Another qualification is mutual respect between partners. For instance, ladies, your man's idea of lovemaking wouldn't be ignoring your calls all day, and then calling you at three in the morning after the club to engage in sexual intercourse. Fellows, your woman's idea of lovemaking wouldn't be based on getting the rent paid next week. Both parties would harbor the good qualities in one another and accept their flaws. Love would be an unselfish and enduring encounter that would take time and constant work.

On the other hand, these days, love is catered to the individual. Again, ladies, your idea of him loving you may be him sending you roses, long walks in the park, writing you sweet love letters, or any other romantic notions that make you feel loved. However, his idea of loving you may have nothing to do with roses, letters, or any of the above. His idea of showing you he loves you could be fixing your car, doing maintenance around your house, or helping your family members with their needs.

Remember, just because someone doesn't love you the way you want them to, doesn't necessarily mean love is non-existent. People are raised with different morals and values, so what mom or dad taught you about love could be totally different from what their parents taught them. If you do find true love, pray about it, cherish it, and KEEP THEM!

Finances…Some people are under the faulty assumption that money isn't a big issue in a relationship. Well, for all of the none believers, it's actually more than a big issue, it's a huge issue. If there are children involved, it could very well be the deal-breaker. Remember that financial troubles contribute to over half of all divorces. Also, keep in mind that financial issues can likely be related to or even a direct result of something that evolved into a more critical situation. Examples of the critical situations that I am referring to are cheating with someone whose financial position is more substantial or getting involved in illegal activities to obtain money, which ultimately may have caused the break-up or divorce. If two people are not financially stable in a relationship, the chance that the relationship will maintain its happiness is slim.

I have heard people say that love determines the relationship. While love is extremely important, you cannot withstand a relationship from love alone. Let's just be honest and ask ourselves, does love bring food to the table and keep a roof over our heads? Does love get your children the supplies and the uniforms they need for school? Did love pay the mortgage last month? No, income from some source does that. Therefore, if you are in a relationship with a person who is a financial burden to your lifestyle, meaning they do not contribute to your basic needs of being financially able to uphold the household, how much love is needed to keep you happy together? Better yet, how much love is needed to keep the relationship surviving at all?

Contrary to what you may believe at this point, I do not feel that money determines the survival of a relationship either. I am sure that Hollywood celebrities have taught you that. What I am saying is that financial stability is just as important as quality time, sex, and communication.

Therefore, it is very important for you and your mate to be aware of what is needed from each of you individually in order to keep the household afloat while not putting too much stress and dependence on the other person. If you are very well off and do not need your lover to contribute to anything financially, then it's not about you needing your lover financially, it is more about your lover needing you. Perhaps you've worked out an agreement where it's more economical for your mate to stay at home with the children. Of course, if you are both wealthy or financially comfortable, then the financial stability in the relationship already exists. Then you may get into what they call a power struggle, which we will discuss at another time. The moral of the story is you have to find some type of financial balance that actually works for both parties.

Women providers…How exactly does a woman play "super hero" to a man? It's time for a true story: I had a friend, I won't mention her name because of legal purposes, but she had a boyfriend who seemed to be a really nice and respectful guy.

He was a mutual friend of a friend, so she knew a little about this guy before they started dating. Getting in depth to his life, he was one call-out away from losing his factory job. He had a few side hustles but did not know what he wanted to do as a career. He ended up losing his job and his apartment, so my friend let him move in with her after three or so months of dating. He was depressed for a few weeks, so my friend started filling out applications for him, helping him with his cell phone bill, gas money, etc., and bought him professional clothes for interviews while trying to encourage him to go back to school. My friend was already in school and working, so she would forget homework assignments and miss classes on his behalf.

She had gotten so involved with this man that she hardly had time to hang with her family. However, she would call and complain to me about how he didn't really know her likes and dislikes. This man didn't even know what she was studying in college.

Meanwhile, one of the jobs from the applications she filled out for him had called him. After working at this job for a few weeks, he didn't offer her any money back for all she had done, and she finally ended up kicking him out for staying out all night on a few occasions. She inevitably found out he was cheating. When it over she didn't understand why he would do that to her after all she had done for him.

Well, the first and most important mistake was that she made everything all about him. It wasn't about what they enjoyed doing as a couple; it was all about her finding him a job and her providing him with resources to get that job. It was about her trying to make him happy instead of trying to have a happy relationship.

You may think she was trying to be a good woman and stand beside her man, and yes, this may have been her intentions, but she got the same results as if she wasn't there helping him. What would have been my suggestion? Of course, filling out his own applications would be a start and he should have had a job before she allowed him to move in with her.

I'm not sure if she offered to pay the cell phone bill or if he asked her, but I would suggest a promissory note if she knew she was going to be paying continuous bills on his behalf. "Thanks Judge Judy." Another factor that's important is if a man doesn't take the time to get to know your likes and dislikes, what excites you or what scares you, and a few of your favorite things, he's really not trying to build anything beyond what you have.

Chapter 6
Leaving Bad Relationships

It is hard to leave a person that you have been with for a while. There may be children involved, both families may be comfortable and familiar with the person, and you don't want to start over with a stranger. Your lover may have good qualities that you once fell in love with, but throughout the relationship, the bad qualities began to outweigh the good on a large scale. Your relationship may be at a point where you two argue every day and sometimes arguments may escalate. Your relationship may also be to a point where you go to work early just to get away from them. The chemistry you had is gone, those butterflies that were in your stomach now cause your stomach to ache when you see them, the sex is more like an arrangement and you sleep in separate rooms. Well, here are just a few reasons to go ahead and throw in the towel.

It will only get worse…How many times have you broken up with a person and they told you they would change or it would get better? Better yet, what did they attempt to do to make this change? Did they go see a psychologist or join a help group? Chances are they stopped that particular behavior for a short period and resumed it as soon as they felt they were back into their comfort zone with you. After you've given them a second or third chance, they have already taken the basics of the behavior and added more to it just to see how much you will tolerate.

A good example of this behavior would be if your partner had jealousy issues in the beginning where he or she would always want to argue and verbally insult you in private has now progressed to public insults and physical altercations. He or she likely didn't want you to have any friends and quite honestly, your friends probably didn't want to be around when they were around. I was in an abusive relationship for years where I experienced this type of treatment, but I stayed in hopes that it would get better.

He was also was emotionally and mentally abusive that subsequently led to physical abusive. I was very young, and I believed that with a little work, he would change for me because of how we (supposedly) love one another so much. Well, he didn't change, and the abuse escalated to a point where I had to get the authorities involved. Point is, the chances of you, alone, changing a person are the same chances you have to hit it big on a lottery ticket.

It will affect the children…There are a lot of couples who feel that staying with each other for the children is the right thing to do regardless of what goes on in the relationship. This is far from the truth. While there may be a convenience factor in that theory, the emotional and psychological affects that bickering parents have on their kids are immense. According to **Hearty House, Inc.**, children who experience domestic disputes in the home are prone to act out with violence or disruptive behavior in school and/or on their siblings. In addition to this, when those children grow up and enter into adult relationships, a good percentage of them carry on what they learned from their parents' examples.

Therefore, history repeats itself in a dreadful cycle.

You deserve to be happy…Although leaving a person you have been with for a long time is hard, you have the right to be happy with the person you are within a relationship. While it is hard to leave a person you have been familiar with for years, you also have to consider the familiarity of verbal, mental, and physical abuse, stress, anxiety, depression or whatever your mate has caused on a continuous basis. If a person makes you feel less than what you are and does not nurture the good qualities and abilities that you have, eventually you'll get to a point where you began to feel miserable about yourself. Your creativity and productivity level decreases, your positive thinking is reverted to negative thoughts, and how you react towards others outside of your relationship, such as family members and co-workers, changes. Life is about the pursuit of happiness and doing constructive things that not only affect you, but those who are around you.

For example, let's go back to the parents' relationship affecting their kids' relationship once they become adults. I know two guys whose parents have both been married roughly 25 to 30 years. Their parents seem to be good Christian people, still laugh together, go out, and have family gatherings…the whole nine. Don't get me wrong, I'm sure they've had their fair share of bumps along the road, but overall, their marriages seem to be decent. Now, back to the sons. Guy one is married, with his own little family, seems happy, goes on family trips and such just like his parents did. However, guy two has no intentions of getting married and even beyond that, long-term **relationships** are non-existent…

I've also seen it the other way around, where children in single parent homes get married and have a successful marriage while some single parent home children never want to get married. Don't get me wrong, I'm not bashing expert professionals by any means. I have a great deal of respect for psychologist who devote themselves to the studies of the human mind and behavioral instincts.

However, I do feel the best advice comes from learned experience. In other words, just because your parents were together or divorced has no bearing on how you will end up in your adult relationship. Although I do agree that we learn as kids from the environment that we grow in, that same environment could have the opposite affect or no factual evidence of an affect at all of how we act as adults in a relationship.

Signs of a Good Relationship Gone Bad

No trust...Do you think your lover has trust issues? Are you aware of the signs that a distrusting companion shows during the relationship? Here are just a few symptoms that overly suspicious partners portray.

Your mate calls every ten minutes...This is one of the most annoying and significant signs that your partner doesn't trust you. In the beginning, you may think this is cute when he or she does it because it could be mistaken as a sign that your mate can't get enough of hearing your voice.

You may think that your conversations are that enduring, or your attention is that heavily needed. Let's be honest, do you really feel a person misses you that much? In actuality, it's a way of knowing who you are with and what you're doing at all times.

Your mate hates when you hang out with your friends…As I briefly discussed earlier, this is an all-time classic sign of a distrusting partner. It becomes even more of a problem if your friends are single. Sometimes lovers will intentionally say negative things about your friends to get you not to hang with them as often or they cause some type of disturbance when you two are together and your friends are around.

This is done to get your friends to not want to be around you, either way your partner wins. I had an ex-boyfriend who would call all my friends whores and make judgments on how they dress and who they dated. Whenever they were in both of our presence, he would make them feel uncomfortable by ignoring them or picking some type of nonsense argument with me.

At times, he even insisted that a few of them tried to get with him at some point. Whether that was true or not, he still went out of his way to disperse any prominent friendships that I had. Needless to say, this relationship didn't last long.

I came to the realization that it wasn't that the poor guy had something against my friends, it was the fact that my friends were attractive and he knew that at some point, he wouldn't be around me with my friends and they would have other men in their social settings who could potentially try to snatch me up. Regardless of the reason, this doesn't give any person the right to disrespect any other relationships or friendships that you may have outside of them.

To sum things up, when your partner tries to get you to ditch your friends, it is likely they are thinking of the possibility that you will meet someone else when you're out with your friends. Obviously, if you have a partner that is insecure within themselves, there is always going to be a trust issue. If the relationship is worth it, talk to your partner. Also, you may want to ask yourself if you've ever given them a reason to feel insecure.

Your partner constantly goes through your belongings…This is probably one of the most obvious signs that your mate has trust issues. In your partner's eyes, it may seem as if things are too good to be true on the surface, therefore, it may be assumed that you are undercover about something.

In order to dig up evidence of deceit, your partner goes through your car, your phone, your wallet/purse, or anything else that personally belongs to you. Typically, a person exhibits this type of behavior when they have been in past **relationships** where they've been cheated on or if you were the cheater at some point of time in the relationship.

If you were the cheater, then there is a good chance that deep down inside, your partner will never trust you, no matter how many times you try to work things out or how many promises you make. Also, your partner could be distrustful because they are doing something wrong and are paranoid that you may be as well. Whatever the issue may be, it is up to you both to decide if the relationship is worth preserving.

Chapter 7&8
Cheating lovers

Sometimes it is hard to tell whether your companion is being faithful or if they had another lover before you two even started dating. Quite honestly, if you are in a long-distance relationship, the chance of your partner cheating is twice as high as being in the same area. However, even if you live over on the next street or in the same home as your lover, if a person wants to cheat, they will cheat. Here are a few signs that tell you that your significant other may not be as committed as they claim. Remember, some situations are circumstantial, and this mainly applies to those who have been dating for a while.

If you have no idea where your partner lives... Although some may not see this as a big deal, it means a lot when a person invites you to their home on several occasions, if not daily.

This not only alleviates the possibility of him or her staying with someone else, but it shows just how much he or she enjoys your company. Just remember, everyone needs their space, so even though you may not accept the offer to see them daily, it's good to know they offered.

If your partner leaves the room every time, he or she gets a phone call... This should be a red-hot sign that your partner has something going on that they obviously don't want you to know about. While some calls may be business related, there are only few select businesses that operate in the wee hours of the morning. Do you get my drift?

They never want to go out to public places unless you two are out of town... The likelihood of this scenario is that your companion is afraid of being seeing by someone who knows him or her that may be related to or friends with their real lover. However, if you happen to see your mate out in public kissing and/or holding hands with another person, you were likely the other woman/man and didn't know it.

Cheating Mates continued…This is one of the most controversial subjects when it comes to relationships. Under what circumstances, if any, should a person accept a cheater back into their life? Is it possible for a cheater to make one or two mistakes or will infidelity always be a part of a cheater's life?

For the most part, no one can really answer these questions because they are all circumstantial. The answers to these questions are going to depend on the ages of the couple, past relationships, the mentality of both parties, and several other factors. There are cases where a person cheats, realizes the mistake that was made and the heartache it caused, and reforms their cheating ways. This is, honestly, rare, but it does happen.

Then, of course, there are the other millions of cases where the cheater is uncaring, selfish, and continues their immoral habits. Since this issue has a general dependency upon the couples' situation, here are some of the risk factors and benefits of taking back a cheater in any relationship.

Risk 1

If you immediately accept a cheater back into your life, he or she will feel it's easy to get you back into the relationship. Most cheaters know who they can manipulate and how. You may become what they call a "push over" meaning you will let your cheating lover treat you less than how you know you should be treated.

Risk 2

The cheater may feel you have a dependency upon them. This dependency could be financial, sexual, or emotional. Once the cheater is comfortable within their self that you need them, all bets are off and your feelings become a playing field.

Risk 3

You are of course risking the chance of getting your heart broken again and we all know that heartache is ten times worse than being punched in the stomach.

More importantly, you're risking the chance of becoming exposed to sexually transmitted diseases due to your partner's infidelity.

Risk 4

You are risking your psychological health as well. Think about it for a minute. When a person cheats, you began to question what is wrong with you or what could you have done better. You question the way you look, how you dressed, the way you acted towards your mate, and several other things when it doesn't have anything to do with you at all.

You may become angry and more aggressive when you deal with others outside of your relationship. In a lot of cases, depression may even submerge. Moreover, probably 99% of jilted lovers compare themselves to the person that their partner cheated with. They want to know what the other person has or what in particular the other person does or doesn't do that captured their lover's attention. It sometimes becomes a mental and emotional exasperation.

Benefits…Unfortunately, there are not too many benefits when accepting a cheater back into your life. Again, in rare cases, the cheater realizes that losing you and/or their family, if you have kids involved, is the worst thing possible and vows that there is no more cheating.

Ultimately, you are still putting your feelings in the hands of your cheating lover. Best-case scenario you have your lover and/or your family back together, but you'll still have doubts regarding his or her honesty and commitment.

So, should you take a cheater back? Well, I have before and guess what? He cheated again and attempted to discover more creative ways to hide his deception. In short, before you decide to get back into a relationship with a cheater, evaluate your personal situation, compare the risks versus the benefits, and make the best decision for you.

Chapter 9
Divorce and Marriage

These days it is hard to decide whether you actually want to get married with a divorce rate that increases almost by the year. Penn State Professor Paul Amato, a nationally renowned expert on parent-child relationships, states that the children of divorced parents are at least 50% more likely to get a divorce than those from an unbroken home according to Smart Marriages, which is a coalition for marriage, family, and couples education. The divorce rate for a second marriage is twice the divorce rate for the first marriage. What's causing this epidemic and what does this mean for individuals who want to re-marry?

There could be plenty of reasons why second marriage divorce rates are higher. For one, in many situations the ex-husband or ex-wife is still in-love with the ex-partner. However, when one partner moves on, it leaves the other partner with no choice but to do the same.

Some people believe by cohabiting with a new lover, that it will help them rid the want and love from their previous companion. In some cases it does, but in most cases it doesn't. Feelings are powerful and undeniable in their own right; therefore, a mere substitution cannot overshadow an authentic emotion. Sometimes the second marriage is already in existence before a person realizes this reality.

Another reason could be contributed to the fact that after the first marriage, a person is less tolerant toward their companion in the second marriage. For example, if the new partner demonstrates some of the same unlikeable characteristics as the previous lover, then that partner is more quickly to opt out because they feel as if history is repeating itself.

On the other hand, if the new lover doesn't have some of the same good qualities or do the good things that the previous partner did, whether it is a sexual, emotional, or physical aspect it sometimes causes withdrawal in the new relationship. What does this mean for those individuals who are already divorced?

Well, I first recommend taking the time to get over your previous partner. If you feel you are over that person, then take time dating before getting into anything else serious. Once you do have a steady partner, learn to appreciate the differences in that partner opposed to criticizing them. Even more importantly, no one is perfect, so work on your flaws and things you may have done that caused deterioration in previous relationships.

Chapter 10
Starting Over/Being Single

The hardest thing to do, at times, is to start over. Whether it's starting a new job, moving into a new house, or starting a new school, new starts are adjustments that take time. Most feel that the best way to get over an ex is to get under another one. The truth of the matter is that getting involved with another person just to get over your ex doesn't necessarily help you get over them. It simply occupies the time that you once spent with that other person or the time that you spend alone thinking of them.

At best, it's another convenient situation for you until you get that ex-lover out of your system. If you truly love someone, feelings do not change overnight. As a matter of fact, depending on the circumstances that ended the departure, you may never truly get over your ex, you just move on because you know you must move on.

Contrary to popular belief, being single isn't that bad. It gives you time to get to know yourself by discovering the things that you like to do. I can honestly say when I was single; I was at my most creative. Why? I didn't have any distractions. I used the time I would have spent on dinner dates, conversations, and going to the movies on research and hobbies that I like. I researched home remedies, do-it-yourself projects, health information, and things about life in general.

In addition to this, I actually wrote the entire rough draft of my first novel, "Partially Broken Never Destroyed" part one in six months. I had time to learn photography, web applications, and other software programs in one year. You probably may think I had a lot of time on my hands, but I actually didn't. I was a full-time college student at Middle Tennessee State University in addition to being a single parent of a newborn.

All in all, before rushing into a different relationship or any relationship, take the time to embrace your potential. Tap into your creativity and if you're not creative, do what you do best. Whether its building things, playing an instrument, singing, or giving advice, explore your given talents. I truly feel that everyone was born with some type of gift or flair; it just takes time to find and discover your niche. To all you out there, best of luck and God Bless.

Works Cited

Smart Marriages, The Coalition for Marriage, Family, and Couple Education (2014 May 10). Retrieved from www.smartmarriages.com